SNOWY & ZOEY' BIG LIFE LESSON

BY HILDA YOUSSEF
PICTURES BY TRENA BRANNON

It was the first day of school for Snowy and Zoey!
Best friends for as long as they can remember.

Summer had been fun. Beach days and ice cream, but school was going to be even better.

Zoey fluttered here and there on the way to school. She was up, up near the sun and then down, down close to Snowy.

The two friends drifted into school singing:
"Ton of fun has begun,
We will run in the sun,
When it's done,
More friends we will have won."

They both had Ms Beary in the blue classroom.

Snowy ran in and found her seat. Zoey fluttered by the door; the classroom looked funny.

Zoey slowly flapped her wings to her seat, her lips trembling and her eyes wide. The classroom looked strange.

Ms Beary said, "Welcome to the blue class. We will all have so much fun together. Do you know this song?

Ton of fun has begun,
We will run in the sun,
When it's done,
More friends we will have won."

Snowy and all her class sang it very loud, again and again. Zoey did not. She kept looking around the room, searching for something.

The animals had painting time. They mixed colors and drew pictures all about their summer fun.

Oliver splashed green! Tommy splashed red! Leila splashed orange! Snowy splashed blue! Maria splashed yellow!

Zoey did not choose a color. Red, green, orange, blue, yellow which one should she take?

Tommy drew the apples he picked from his grandpa's tree.

Oliver drew the green trees of the forest he had walked through with his brother.

Leila drew the orange flowers she had planted with her mother in the garden.

Snowy drew the blue sea she had splashed in with Zoey.

Maria drew the sunset she had watched with her sister.

Finally, Zoey took the red paint and drew the firetruck she had ridden on at the fire station.

Ms Beary asked the students to sit on the carpet for circle time.

Zoey loved circle time.

Ms Beary clapped the tune, and the animals started singing:

"Ton of fun has begun,
We will run in the sun,
When it's done,
More friends we will have won."

Ms Beary asked the animals to share with the class their hobbies.

Snowy loved to read mystery books.

Oliver loved to play the drums.

Maria loved to do karate.

Tommy loved to play tennis.

Leila loved to make outdoor art.

Zoey loved to do karate, too.

Ms Beary said, "It is wonderful to see that Zoey and Maria both enjoy Karate."

It was break time! Who doesn't love break time?!

The animals ran out to the playground, laughing and screaming.

Snowy told Zoey to hurry up! The playground was full of fun things to do.

Maria was bouncing a ball here and there.

Oliver was drawing with sidewalk chalk.

Tommy was on the monkey bars.

Leila was on the slide.

Snowy was playing with a hula hoop.

Zoey happily fluttered near Oliver and joined him in some chalk fun.

The end of the school day had come! Time to say goodbye to Ms Beary and all their new friends.

Snowy and Zoey made their way home. Snowy was skipping excitedly, "What a great day we had, Zoey, don't you think?"

Zoey looked at Snowy and smiled, "When we entered the blue classroom, I felt different and sad. I wanted to cry. Everyone there did not look like me. They had a different color and could not fly.

As the school day ended, I understood that we are all different but have plenty in common too!"

Snowy laughed, "You are my best friend in the whole world, Zoey. We don't look the same, and we don't sound the same, isn't that what makes us special?"

The End.

CPSIA information can be obtained
at www.ICGtesting.com
Printed in the USA
LVRC102300040122
707895LV00002B/9